THE RUM RUNNERS

by FRANK W. ANDERSON

*Honorable Arthur L. Sifton, premier of
Alberta when prohibition became law.*

ISBN 0-919214-11-8
Copyright © 1968 Frontier Publishing Ltd. and
Copyright © 1980 Heritage House Publishing Company Ltd.

FRONTIER BOOKS
Box 1228, Station A
Surrey, B.C. V3S 2B3

Printed in Canada

FOREWORD

"The liquor traffic is of such a nature that when you squeeze it in one place, it seems to break out in another."

— Hon. J. R. Boyle,
Attorney General

Illicit still near Cardston in the early 1920s.

The photo above shows the bar in the Alberta Hotel in Crossfield between 1908-13 and, below, the Assiniboia Hotel bar about 1914.

THE DAMP DAYS

"Sorry, gentlemen, no more drinks. We haven't a drop left."

By 10 o'clock on that Friday evening, June 30th, 1916, there wasn't a drop of legal liquor to be purchased in Calgary, Edmonton, Lethbridge, Red Deer or Medicine Hat. Since 7 o'clock that night, quiet groups of citizens had been moving from bar to bar, from hotel to favorite hotel, solemnly having "Another one against the drought ahead." Everyone seemed in a cheerful mood, as if Prohibition were a huge joke and as if legislation could change the fundamental nature of man. The streets were filled with automobiles, moving slowly along, the passengers either part of the jovial mob of "last nighters" or part of the horde of non-drinking, interested spectators. By 11 o'clock, the patient police had carted off the last unstable reveller and the streets were clear.

It was all like some wonderful prank. It was a marvelous idea to swear off drinking for the duration of the war. But, no one really knew what lay ahead.

In some parts of the province, it was a different story. Through the Crows Nest Pass, in towns like Coleman, Blairmore and Frank; in St. Albert, Bon Accord and Morinville, north of Edmonton, the mood of the "last nighters" was different. "I've been drinking beer since I was old enough to jump over a miner's lamp," said Joe Perotte, "And I'm damned if I'm gonna stop now."

Nevertheless, when the clock struck midnight and the world moved into the new day of July 1st, 1916, Prohibition was in force — and many a citizen slipped down into the cellar to take stock of his spirits against the coming ordeal of thirst.

No one was really sure where the idea started. In February, 1914, the Temperance and Moral Reform League of Alberta had decided to approach the government to hold a plebiscite on Prohibition, basically to curtail the misuse of alcoholic beverages. Public drunkenness was common and the social problems arising from intemperate drinking were enormous. It was estimated that 90% of the cases appearing in police courts had a solid causation of alcoholism. It seemed quite logical to assume that by preventing people from drinking, these evils would disappear.

On October 9th, 1914, Premier Sifton moved that the Prohibition bill be submitted direct to the electors and the motion was passed. It was decided to hold the plebiscite on July 21st, 1915.

As 1915 opened, a lively campaign began. Heading the drive for Prohibition was the executive of the Temperance League: President T. H. Miller; General Secretary W. F. Gold; Campaign Manager

A. W. Coone; Treasurer J. H. MacDonald and Finance Chairman A. T. Cushing. Speakers of the calibre of Clinton N. Howard of Rochester, N.Y., and Ben S. Spence of Toronto were brought in to condemn the evils of drinking, and these were ably supported by the exhortations of such local orators as Reverend F. W. Patterson, First Baptist Church, Edmonton, and celebrated authoress, Nellie McClung.

The Licensed Victuallers Association of Alberta, who were against the misuse of liquor but in favor of freedom of drinking, imported C. A. Windle of Chicago and advertised intelligently in local newspapers, but they were clearly out-gunned, out-shouted and out-thought by the Dries. As a result, it was no contest, and on July 21st, 1915, the people of Alberta endorsed Prohibition (or rather their individual concept of it) by a whopping majority of 21,086.

NELLIE McCLUNG

Significantly, the coal mining towns of the Pass, as well as Lethbridge, Bow Valley and Pincher Creek voted Wet. In the northern portion of the province, St. Paul, Victoria and St. Albert voted Wet.

The date was set — July 1st, 1916.

The Act, when published, was an enormous piece of legislation, filled with "whereas" and clause and sub-section, and it is really doubtful whether anyone in the whole province — including its authors — was competent to interpret it. Basically, it provided that after July 1st, 1916, all beer parlours and liquor houses would be closed and that no liquor might be purchased or sold in the province unless the purpose was medicinal, scientific or sacred. Among the 11 pages of closely printed rules and regulations was a provision to establish government vendor stores to meet the medicinal, sacrificial and scientific needs of the community, and it is interesting to note that Rev. W. F. Gold, erstwhile secretary of the Moral Reform League, was appointed to the post of Vendor in Edmonton. In Calgary, the only other major outlet opened, another minister, Rev. John McDougall, was appointed liquor vendor at a salary of $1,800 per annum.

Provision was also made that a "Temperance Beer", containing less than 2½% of alcohol, might be sold, and all the major breweries began to produce these. Possibly the most appropriate name for these mild beers was the one chosen by Calgary Brewing and Malting Company: "Chinook".

Having gained the passage of "their law", the Moral Reform League next addressed its energies towards securing strict enforcement of the provisions of the Act. Well aware that local police forces were short handed because of the World War I drain on manpower, and conscious that extreme community pressure could be brought to bear upon enforcement officers in outlying, or closely knit communities, the League began agitation for the creation of a politically independent commission to enforce Prohibition.

LOOPHOLES

It quickly became evident that the 1916 Act had loopholes big enough to drive a beer truck through. Although Saskatchewan had gone dry on July 1st, 1915, and Manitoba had installed Prohibition on July 1st, 1916, British Columbia was still wet. Also, the United States was permitting the free sale of intoxicants, and while the border was guarded by Mounted Police and Customs officials, these guardians were few and far between and the early rum-runners had little or no difficulty evading detection.

Actually, however, there was little need for rum-running, that is, the transportation of liquor from the manufacturer to the distributors,

7

or for the creation of illicit whiskey stills. The Act permitted Albertans to import liquor for their personal use. The only restriction was, that while **medicine** purchased for treatment could be carried anywhere by the patient, liquor imported from out of the province could only be maintained in a dwelling. Further, the Act set a limit of 1 quart of hard liquor or 1 gallon of malt spirits (beer) that might be kept in a private or other dwelling.

While it was true that 58,295 had voted for Prohibition, 37,209 had voted against it. Evidently, the latter were determined to have their nip.

A steady stream of liquor flowed into the province. John Allen, waiter on the C.P.R., was but one of many railwaymen who brought back liquor from Golden, B.C., in their travelling cases. Local police in Calgary, Edmonton and Macleod were forever raiding dining cars and seldom failed to find a private cache. While hotel bars were closed — resulting in many hotels going out of business — the private citizen had only to send in an order to the export warehouses, which sprang up miraculously in Fernie and Golden in British Columbia, and in Maple Creek, Regina and Saskatoon in Saskatchewan, and have his parcel delivered to the local Dominion Express office. So brisk did this import business become that the Express companies were compelled to set up separate offices to handle the volume.

An effective system soon evolved. Liquor manufacturers in Alberta shipped their products to liquor export concerns in Saskatchewan and British Columbia. Breweries in Saskatchewan shipped to export houses in Alberta. The private citizen in Alberta or Saskatchewan simply ordered from the neighboring province. In order to circumvent the provision that a person might have only 1 quart of hard liquor or 1 gallon of beer on hand, astute buyers placed standing orders with the export companies to forward a steady stream of daily parcels, each of which conformed to government regulations.

The only serious attempt to defeat the law by force came on October 11th, 1916, when soldiers from Calgary's Sarcee barracks staged a protest riot. Smarting from the lack of liquor and annoyed by the fact that many of them had been prevented from voting in the plebiscite because of delays and residential requirements, the men in khaki expressed their disapproval by street fighting and destruction.

On the less violent side, Edmonton lawyer G. E. Winkler, appearing before Magistrate Philip Primrose on behalf of Mon Yuen, who was charged with having 2 gallons of liquor in his possession, declared that the people of Alberta had no right to create an Act by plebiscite and that therefore the Prohibition Act was illegal.

In a decision handed down on February 6th, 1917, Magistrate Primrose (who had just been appointed to head a provincial force to suppress liquor) declared that the Act was legal, dismissed the argument and found Mon Yuen guilty.

The first season of Prohibition rolled merrily along, with sufficient drinks to appease the thirsts of the dissenters. Distilleries kept up their regular rate of production, freight trains rolled across the borders of Saskatchewan and British Columbia with consignments of liquor, and express trains transported the same liquids back across the same borders in neatly packaged, legal parcels. There was a sudden appreciation of the value of hard liquor as a medicinal remedy for almost every ailment known to man, and the government vendors and breweries were kept busy supplying drugstores across the province with liquor to meet the prescriptions filled in for patients by doctors. Strangely, the dosage required for each treatment was 40 ounces!

CREATION OF THE A.P.P.

During the first year of Prohibition, enforcement of the intent of the Act was subdivided between three bodies of officials. In the larger cities and towns, where a police force existed, the task fell to them. In the rural areas and smaller villages, the R.N.W.M. Police — their ranks decimated by war enlistments — carried on the job. The burden of ferreting out illicit whiskey stills and of prosecuting the operators fell to agents of the Inland Revenue Department, a federal agency.

The Moral Reform League were constantly agitating for the creation of a liquor enforcement body, but the provincial government was holding firm — primarily because of the costs involved. Then, suddenly, to the consternation of Premier A. L. Sifton (and the delight of the Moral Reform League) a Dominion Order In Council was passed on November 29th, 1916, providing for the cancellation of the services of the Mounted Police after March 1st, 1917. This meant that the R.N.W.M. Police would be withdrawn from rural police duty in the province and this action would create a gaping hole in protective and preventive police services.

Premier Sifton made several valiant attempts to have their services retained, but failed. He then turned his attention to the creation of a provincial police force to fill the void which would be created. His task was made even more difficult by the war-time shortage of emergency funds in provincial coffers.

On February 3rd, 1917, he announced that Magistrate Philip Primrose, Edmonton; Gilbert Sanders, Calgary magistrate; and Deputy Attorney General Browning would form a Provincial Police Commission to have charge of the new force. Mr. Primrose would be chairman of the Commission. Four days later, Mr. Sifton appointed Major A. E. C. McDonnell, then Superintendent of Mounted Police at Athabasca, as the first Chief of the force.

9

Three days after his appointment to head the Alberta Provincial Police Commission, Mr. Primrose, in his other capacity of Magistrate, thoughtfully handed down the decision on the Mon Yuen case, declaring that the Act he had to uphold as Commissioner of Police was legal. Opposition members in the Legislature cried: "Dirty pool!", but it did them no good.

The first Deputy Chief of the A.P.P. was John Daniel Nicholson. Nicholson was one of the fabulous characters of the Old Canadian West. Joining the N.W.M.P. at Halifax in 1885, he was posted west and saw service at Regina, Edmonton and the Crows Nest Pass. He assisted in several early important arrests, among these the apprehension of "Cracker Box" Johnson, card sharp and whiskey runner from Montana. His most famous case was the determined manhunt and eventual conviction of killer William Oscar King in 1910. He had retired from the Mounted Police on pension on March 15th, 1911, to assume the post of Chief of Detectives for the Attorney General's Department.

To him fell the main burden of organizing and recruiting the new force. Says Nicholson: "the organization of the A.A.P. (Alberta Provincial Police) took place in my office and the first 100 men were sworn in by myself."

Though the Act creating the A.P.P. had not yet been passed, the force came into being on March 1st, 1917. By then, 96 men had been screened and accepted. It was a difficult task, with most of the able-bodied men in the army, and recruits were lured from the ranks of local police forces or pressed back into service after retirement from the Mounted Police. Indicative of the haste with which the force had been assembled was the fact that when they moved into make-shift barracks, they were minus equipment, had only a handful of horses, 3 Ford motor cars and no uniforms.

However, by April 20th, the A.P.P. was nearly ready. Uniforms were on order and men were being posted to outlying detachments. A state of mild confusion had finally emerged from the initial chaos, and the police were ready to enforce the laws — including the Liquor Act.

Fortunately, there was no serious crime wave during the first month of disorganization. The only ripple came on the night of April 28th, when John Paul Ryan and George McIntyre robbed the St. Albert branch of the Banque de Hochelaga. The A.P.P. rose to the occasion and had the culprits behind bars within 48 hours.

Even when fully up to strength, which comprised 125 men, including a Superintendent, a Deputy Superintendent, 5 Inspectors, and the balance of Sergeants, Detectives and Constables, the task of the A.P.P. in liquor control was almost impossible. It had an entirely new personnel, there was a total lack of any traditions, and in some cases of morale, and it worked under the fierce spotlight of surveillance that beats on every new endeavour. They functioned under extreme difficulty. For example, "C" Division, with headquarters at Calgary, had 33 men and officers to patrol an area which stretched from Bowden on the north to Cayley on the south, and east and west to the provincial borders. The 22,000 square miles involved worked out to about 700 square miles per man. To cover this expanse of prairie, foothills and mountains, they had 15 horses and 3 Model "T" Ford cars.

Nevertheless, the A.P.P. was active at the most awkward moments.

Mr. Joseph Silbernagel, a respected farmer who lived 7 miles southwest of Beiseker, had stocked up 5 quarts of good whiskey and 117 bottles of beer for the wedding of his daughter. At the most inopportune time — just before the celebrations — Detective E. I. Schoeppe, assisted by Constables McLear and Mellally, swooped down on the Silbernagel farm and confiscated the lot.

The A.P.P. were scarcely settled into their saddles before two events took place which increased the difficulties under which they had to operate. On July 1st, 1917, in response to constant prodding from the Social Service League (successor to the old Moral

J. D. NICHOLSON

Reform League), the government created new and more stringent amendments to the Liquor Act. It was now forbidden for **anyone** to have in their possession more than 1 quart of liquor or 2 gallons of beer. This restriction applied equally to private citizens and business concerns. The amendments also provided for the police to inspect freight and express company books and records.

The restriction in the amount of liquor that might be kept on hand meant the death of the liquor warehouses, but it also created a rather unexpected problem. When the law came into effect on July 1st, 1917, all the warehouses had a considerable quantity of stocks on hand. These had to be disposed of. Unfortunately, the Dominion Express Company and the railways were also affected by the act and could not accept bulk shipments to clear the warehouses! They, likewise, might only have 1 quart of liquor or 2 gallons of beer on hand.

Nevertheless, by midnight, July 3rd (allowing 3 days of grace because of the Dominion Holiday), the liquor warehouses were empty.

An enterprising **Calgary Herald** reporter questioned Mr. W. J. Tulk, manager of the Gold Seal Liquor Company, with regard to the disposal of stock, but received no answer. It later developed that many companies had merely moved their stocks out of the central warehouses and were storing them in icehouses, garrets, stables and basements. Some managed to spirit their liquor away in trucks and disposed of them in United States, and even as far away as China.

Technically, the new amendments were designed to assist the supression of the liquor trade, but as time proved, they in effect created new headaches for the A.P.P.

The closing of the Alberta liquor export warehouses actually hurt the residents of Saskatchewan and British Columbia, for it meant that they could no longer have orders shipped from Alberta to their homes. Since the export warehouses in Saskatchewan and British Columbia were still operating, Alberta breweries could still ship their produce outside the province and the Albertans could still have it imported back.

While British Columbia adopted a modified version of Prohibition on July 1st, 1917, liquor was not difficult to obtain. Besides, Montana was still wide open. A moderate amount of rum-running between Montana-Utah and the provinces of Alberta and British Columbia sprang into being, but it was not serious. Import liquor was still readily available and the steady flow of prescription **medicine** kept the temperatures of the drinkers at tolerable levels.

There was a steady upsurge in the sale of patent medicines and food flavouring extracts, such as vanilla, following July 1st, 1917. All of these contained more than 2½% of alcohol allowed

12

by the Act, and by August 23rd, the government was compelled to pass an Order forbidding the sale of these without a prescription from a doctor. Grocers were forbidden to carry them in stock, and they could only be obtained from a druggist who had a license to handle liquor.

Hard hit by this ruling was Tuxedo Coffee and Spice Mills, the only manufacturer of flavouring extracts in the province. The spirit content of their extracts varied from 51% to 90%, the average being 77%. As these extracts could only be sold through drug stores and under prescription, housewifes soon refused to purchase a $1.00 prescription from their doctor to cover the purchase of a 25 cent bottle of extract. A modest business in illicit extract sales to housewives sprang up, but the over-all sales dropped off.

The law relating to the sale of extracts was found to be unworkable in certain areas of the province where there were no drug stores. Government agents were forced to look the other way and did not prosecute grocers who carried reasonable supplies of the extracts on their shelves.

Prohibition seemed to be creating more headaches than it prevented.

Cars of the 20's

A.P.P. Men With a Haul

14

However, despite these new regulations, Alberta was still "quite damp". It was the opinion of the A.P.P. that large quantities of liquor were being brought into the province in sealed trunks, suitcases and other packages.These were sent by train to points along the line where there was no A.P.P. detachment and from thence to their final destinations. A favorite device for bulk shipments was to send them in boxcars labelled "household furniture". Express company officials admitted that there "might be a bit of this" but felt it was limited. Here and there a small whiskey still sprang into operation; here and there a car scurried furtively across the United States border; here and there a friendly doctor prescribed "the medicine" freely.

By the end of 1917, the police of Alberta were convinced that their efforts to enforce the law were only creating more lawlessness. They felt that bootlegging — the actual selling transaction to the consumer — and the illicit manufacture of liquor were steadily increasing, and, since the law provided only fines as penalties, there was little hope of suppressing the trade unless the law was changed to provide imprisonment as well. In Calgary alone, for example, the number of liquor cases jumped from 127 in 1916 to 346 in 1917.

Mt. T. C. H. Primrose, Chairman of the Police Commission, in direct contradiction to what his field officers were saying, scoffed at the idea that bootlegging was on the increase or that any difficulty should be met in stamping out the trade. "Trail the town drunkard and he will lead you to the still," Primrose advocated in a piece of cracker-barrel philosophy. However, the "town drunk" wasn't as evident as he had been in the old days. Supt. P. W. Pennefather, R.N.W.M.P., Lethbridge, commented on the Alberta picture unofficially: "there is now almost a total absence of drunkenness in public places."

Up until the end of 1917, it would seem that the situation was not bothersome on either side. The citizen still continued to obtain ample supplies of spirits without undue effort and the police made the necessary raids on cafe, laundry and pool room.

One faction was not happy with the "status quo" and continued to apply steady pressure through submissions to the government for stricter enforcement of the law. This was the Social Service League, successor to the Moral Reform League. In its zeal to assist in stamping out the liquor traffic, the League sent out circulars in the fall of 1917, asking citizens to report liquor offences to them. Report forms, printed secretly in Winnipeg, asked for details of alleged offences known to the citizen. There were places on the forms for the name of the offender, the place, the date, names of confirmatory witnesses, and whether the offence had been reported to the police. These forms were sent out to all citizens with the request that they complete them and return them — not to their local police — but to the General Secretary of the League at 714 Tegler Block in Edmonton. Officials were quick to observe that this tactic could be used to check on the efficiency of the various police forces.

Across the face of the province, the whole liquor question was treated with lightness. Citizens clucked their tongues when "Jolting Joe", the local bootlegger, appeared in court for a fine of $50.00 and costs, and wondered how soon he would be back in business for them. There was no extensive, furious campaign by the undermanned police to stamp out the evil. Liquid refreshments were not impossible to obtain, just "difficult".

PRESSURE BUILDS UP

Suddenly, on the night of February 27th, 1918, violence entered the picture.

Having received information from informers that a gang of thieves would attempt to remove whiskey from some boxcars in the C.P.R. freight yards at Calgary that night, Det. Sgt. James Murray and Constable E. W. Sawyer of the C.P.R. police stationed themselves in the yard. For some time, there had been numerous petty thefts of whiskey from the cars.

About 8:30 p.m., a car containing Arthur King and Harry Ellis, two well-known local characters, together with several other men, drew up near the tracks. They were joined by another man and all approached a freight car and began to carry out cases and cartons.

As the police moved in to apprehend the men, Arthur King started up the car and raced off. Constable Sawyer later stated that he was shooting at the car and that his bullets went wild and struck a member of the gang, Buckley K. Bradley. Bradley, wounded twice in the neck and face, fled towards the National Hotel, with Det. Sgt. Murray in pursuit.

Inspector Brankley, A.P.P., who happened to be in the vicinity, heard the shooting and drove to the scene just in time to have the severely wounded man collapse in his arms.

After spending some weeks in critical condition in the hospital, Bradley was brought to trial on May 29th, and a very different picture began to emerge. The evidence indicated that Bradley, a C.P.R. switchman, 23, married, had been on his way to his home in East Calgary, and that he had hitched a ride on a passing freight train. When he saw some cases lying beside the railroad tracks, he had jumped off and had picked one up to carry to a place of security in the nearby freight sheds. He had only gone about 150 feet

16

when he was accosted by Det. Sawyer, who shot him twice at close range without warning. He then ran, as he said, to save his life.

After deliberating less than half an hour, the jury returned a not-guilty verdict in his favour.

The whole incident made serious-minded citizens wonder. Were they, and officialdom, fooling themselves? Were they in effect walking on the thin crust of a volcano that could erupt? The police were under steady criticism for their failure to stamp out liquor; there was a good number of citizens who intended to obtain their "blue ruin"; and there were men who desired, for various reasons, to supply the grog. In such a situation, too much pressure on such a gaseous subject, could only create an explosion.

It seemed that the Social Service League intended, intentionally or otherwise, to supply that pressure.

With an abundance of liquor still flowing in the province, The Social Service League was beginning to see its victory as a hollow thing. It began, through its president, J. A. Virtue, to exert more pressure upon the government for more stringent rules and more effective enforcement. Prime target was the A.P.P. It was acknowledged that there was discontent in the force and disunity between the field officers and the three-man Police Commission. Deputy Superintendent Nicholson had already resigned in disgust, and on March 26th, the Superintendent, A. E. C. McDonnell, resigned for reasons of "ill health". He was replaced by Lt. Colonel G. E. Bryan. Since the creation of the force, there had been 66 resignations, 14 men had been dismissed and 4 of these under a cloud of suspicion connected with illicit liquor traffic.

In the Legislature, A. F. Ewing, opposition member from West Edmonton, and George Hoadley, M.L.A. from Okotoks and leader of the opposition, demanded a full investigation of the A.P.P. and the return of the Mounted Police to active duty throughout Alberta.

Defending the right of the Provincial Police to work out their problems without political interference, the Premier stuck to his guns and the moves were defeated. There were indications, however, that important changes would be made in the police force.

On March 14th, a strong delegation of Social Service League members, headed by Rev. A. W. Coone, met with Premier Charles Stewart and demanded that a fourth commissioner be appointed to the A.P.P. to have full responsibility to enforce the Act. They wanted the A.P.P. increased in strength and a special squad of plainclothes men created for a liquor detail. They demanded the return of the government vendor stores — which had been forced out of business by competition from druggists and importers — and the imposition of jail sentences for chronic offenders. Most dangerous of all their demands was the request that the need for warrants of search or arrest in liquor offences should be abolished.

A week later, new amendments to the Liquor Act were presented in the Legislature and these echoed faithfully the demands of the Social Service League.

As finally approved, the 1918 amendments provided a clearer definition of the product they were trying to suppress — namely, any liquid containing over 2½% of alcohol, whether used as a beverage or not. It provided that all persons privileged to have liquor stocks, such as druggists, scientists, ministers of the gospel, must purchase these from the government vendor, and that henceforth accurate records of stock purchased, on hand and sold, must be maintained. It also gave the A.P.P. increased powers to inspect the premises and records of any person dealing with liquor.

One bitterly fought amendment revolved around the Social Service League sponsored proposal that the police have the authority to arrest "on suspicion" without a warrant. Yielding to the strong protests of Lt. Frank Walker, Victoria riding, and A. F. Ewing, West Edmonton, that this was a dangerous precedent and smacked of persecution rather than prosecution, the government dropped its attempt to include this police-state measure.

Events outside the Alberta Legislature were also conspiring to make the life of the Alberta tippler more difficult. On December 22nd, 1917, the Dominion government announced that after December 24th, no liquor or beverage containing more than 2½% of alcohol could be imported into Canada and, that after April 1st, 1918, no one might ship liquor from one province to another. This provision was a death blow to the export liquor business. This federal measure was designed to further the war effort and was to remain in force for 12 months after the conclusion of peace.

The combined effort of the Dominion Order in Council banning importation of liquor and the new stringent regulations regarding the sale of liquor within the province of Alberta, was to force the liquor traffic to go underground. It paved the way for the large scale rum-runner and the operator of the big illicit still.

THE RISE OF THE RUM RUNNER

With Montana still permitting the free sale of liquor, it was natural that the focus point of the rum running industry would be in the south. There were three main centers of operation.

At Lethbridge, the business was conducted by a tall, well-dressed and distinguished looking garage man, Mr. R . . . It was said that he came originally from the Edmonton area, where he had operated a tavern before prohibition. He seemed to bear a charmed

EMILIO PICARIELLO

life, for he was never apprehended, and ugly rumors in the community linked his name closely with that of high government officials on both sides of the Canadian-U.S. border. He received his liquor in carload lots — most of it the product of legitimate distilleries — and hid this on the farms of various friends in the community. From these secret caches, he transported the liquor by means of two Cadillacs, one Maxwell, and an Olds. The latter was registered in the name of his garage. His closest competitor was George F . . . who operated two McLaughlins as well as a Ford truck.

The second major point of distribution was the Alberta Hotel. in Blairmore, owned and operated by the fabulous Emilio Picariello, affectionately known as Mr. Pick, the Bottle King. As early as 1917. someone gave him the name of Emperor Pick, because of his widespread operations — legitimate and otherwise.

Emilio Picariello, born in Sicily in 1875, was beyond doubt the most fabulous personality to emerge on the Prohibition scene. Immigrating to Canada around the turn of the century, he settled first in Toronto, where he worked as an electrician. Here he met Marian, a comely Italian girl just over from Italy. They were married in Toronto and subsequently purchased a small confectionary store and began to raise a family of seven, the eldest of whom was Steve.

In 1911, Mr. Pick moved his family to Fernie, B,C., where he obtained employment in the Macaroni Factory, operated by G. Maraniro, and later, when Maraniro moved to Lethbridge to open a new factory, Mr. Pick took charge of the Fernie branch.

A big man, 5'-8" and tipping the scales at nearly 200 pounds, Emilio had a huge zest for life and and amazing capacity for work. He had a wonderful ability to make friends, and an intense, inquiring mind that was ever alert to intriguing business possibilities. A kind man, he loved bluster and intrigue, but at the same time had that indefinable quality which made people trust him.

He also seemed destined by fate to become involved in the liquor business, and the question was whether he followed the liquor business, or whether it followed him.

In February, 1912, for example, Mr. Pick was raising his double cottage, preparatory to putting a foundation and cellar beneath it. The house was jacked up on beer barrels. About 7:00 p.m. Sunday evening, February 18th, one of the barrels caved in and the house lurched sideways, wedging between the adjacent buildings. All the windows were broken and the entire structure was badly twisted. Fortunately, no one was injured.

The editor of the **Fernie Free Press** jokingly pointed out that: "a beer barrel will carry considerable weight but has never been famous for stability."

20

Among Mr. Pick's closest friends and gambling companions was Mr. P. Carosella, the local wholesale liquor merchant. It was therefore not surprising that by December 1914, Mr. Pick was completely in the liquor business as the local representative for the Pollock Wine Company.

For the next two years, Mr. E. Pick went quietly about building up the business at the Macaroni Factory. He tried manufacturing cigars; he developed a large foodstuffs business, with such sidelines as the sale of Timothy hay. By March, 1916, he had branched out into the manufacture of ice cream and could produce 400 gallons a day. He put an ice-cream wagon on the streets of Fernie that summer, and within a year he had established ice-cream parlours in both Blairmore, Alberta, and Trail, B.C.

As another interesting sideline, Emilio began to collect bottles. At first, the community merely smiled tolerantly at this seeming eccentricity, for Pick was a well-liked celebrity, but gradually it became apparent that something was happening to the beer bottle industry.

On September 22nd, 1916, he advertised 27,000 bottles for sale; quarts 40 cents, pints 22 cents a dozen. Unassumingly, the big, smiling man had gained a monopoly on bottles and the local breweries soon found it cheaper to rely on his efficient bottle-gathering system than to try to collect their own or buy new ones. Thereafter, his ad appeared regularly in newspapers throughout the Pass: "E. Pick, the Bottle King, requests that all persons selling bottles hold them until they see E. Pick, who pays top prices."

When prohibition came to Alberta in 1916, Mr. Pick, as agent for the Pollock Wine Company, moved quickly into the export business and began to make money.

In January, 1918, Mr. Pick purchased the Alberta Hotel in Blairmore from Fritz Sick, of the Lethbridge Brewing Company, and moved his family from Fernie. The people of Fernie remembered him for his many little acts of generosity, for his eccentricities — like the winter of 1913 when he and his business associate, Charles Lassandro, captured a full-grown wolf and brought him back to town on a chain; for his activities in the local Italian community; and for the little black bear that was sometimes chained up at the door to the Macaroni Factory.

Mr. Pick also remembered his friends and business associates in Fernie.

On March 1st, 1918, Emilio Picariello became sole agent for Fritz Sick's Lethbridge Brewery products in the Crows Nest Pass, and, with that touch of showmanship that seemed so natural to him his advertisements in the Pass newspapers featured "temperance drinks".

With the declaration of "total prohibition" in Alberta on April

21

Picariello, Lassandro and Friend

1st, 1918, thanks to the stoppage of inter-provincial shipments of liquor, Mr. Pick, along with others, was quick to see the business possibilities of running liquor into southern Alberta. The people of the Pass welcomed him with open arms and freely aided and abetted his new venture.

Starting with "Model T" Fords, Mr. Pick began supplying the needs of the community. To cope with the occasional police road barrier, he equipped his Fords with bumpers made from piping filled with concrete. He loved the hazard, the bravado, the sensationalism and the prestige it gave him. He used the Alberta Hotel as the legitimate front for his rum running activities. Towards the end of 1918, he traded in his "Model T" Fords for the faster, more compact McLaughlins.

Preparatory to opening his sideline, Mr. Pick excavated a small room off the basement and from this room he extended a tunnel a short distance out under the roadway. The entrance to this side room was usually covered with burlap sacking, and in front of this rough curtain were several large barrels in which were stored empty 40 ounce bottles. A favorite device for bringing in liquor was to load trucks with flour. The outer layers of sacks contained flour — in case of a search — but behind this innocent wall were burlap sacks containing bottles of the illicit booze. The trucks were able to drive right under the building to deposit their dual loads. The liquor was concealed in the tunnel and the flour was distributed to needy families in the town.

One of Mr. Pick's prized possessions was a player piano which stood in the hotel lounge. When played loudly, as it usually was, it served to drown out the noise of the activity in the basement.

The contraband liquor was obtained from friends in Fernie, and it is interesting to note the regularity with which the Fernie Exporters Company Limited, and the B.C. Export Company appeared in the Fernie magistrate's court to pay stiff fines for infractions of the B.C. Liquor Act.

As he became more affluent, Mr. Pick subscribed for $50,000 in Canadian Victory Bonds to help the war effort, and gave freely to the poor at Christmas time. The editor of the Blairmore **Enterprise** remarked that it was surprising how many "poor" families suddenly appeared each Christmas.

It was Emilio's boast that he could place his hands on a large sum of cash at a moment's notice, and once, to prove his point to an old friend, Tony Andrea, he reached into his car, picked up a wad of dirty rags from the floorboards and unwrapped $3,000 in bills.

In Fernie, the Mr. Big of the rum runners was also a garage man. He was alleged to have gotten his start on a loan of $1,000 from Emilio Picariello; and it was said that he obtained his supplies

23

from an export company which occupied the building which now houses the Fernie Dairy adjacent to the tracks. Employing several drivers, Mr. Big competed with Mr. Pick for the Crows Nest Pass business. Because of police surveillance, he established several hide-outs along the Pass road into which the cars could be taken and the illicit cargo be removed to a place of hiding. One of these secret caches was at a garage in Lundbreck. The garage contained a well and part way down the well, a tunnel led off underneath the building. Though the well was searched several times by members of the A.P.P., the existence of the tunnel was not suspected and is still in reasonable operating condition to this day.

The liquor from the Fernie operators and from the caches of Mr. R . . . and George F . . . in the Lethbridge area was quite often transshipped to other rum runners in central and northern Alberta. These latter operators, such as M. D. Sopper, Thomas McLaughlin and S. A. Whitman, brought the whiskey in by car along the old Macleod Trail through High River and Okotoks to Calgary. Jack Redford, another of the runners, preferred to come into Calgary by going north from Lethbridge to a point near Strathmore and then turning west along the main highway. A favorite tactic of these operators was to rent cars from Webbers Garage in the foothills city, carry out their flying trips to Montana or Lethbridge, and return the rented car at the completion of the trip.

Sopper-McLaughlin-Whitman operated quite effectively until the afternoon of October 15th, 1918, when they were apprehended by members of the A.P.P. just south of Okotoks. The two Ford cars and their cargos were seized and confiscated by the government. Jack Redford met a similar fate a month later when his two Fords were stopped and seized near Langdon. However, with the enormous profits to be made from illegal liquor, the $500 fines levied in each instance were no real deterrent and all men were shortly back in operation.

The restriction on imported liquor also made the manufacture of illicit beverages profitable and worth the risk for the first time since the establishment of Prohibition.

On August 30th, 1918, Calgary Chief Police Alfred Cuddy received a tip from the local military authorities that an empty store on 17th Avenue West would bear investigation. The attention of the military had been drawn to the building by an anonymous caller who was certain that the men seen around the empty building were plotting to undermine the sidewalk and blow up a streetcar full of soldiers from the nearby barracks.

Arriving at the duplex building, one side of which housed a gospel hall meeting house, Cuddy and his men swooped in and caught Charles Pace, a bootblack, and J. H. Von Koolbergen, local mystery man, busily engaged in drawing off a batch of malt beer. The store had been rented by Von Koolbergen a few weeks before as a furniture storage room and the windows had been boarded up. Behind these wooden curtains, the two had carried on an extensive bootleg manufacturing business capable of turning out 75 gallons a week at $15.00 a gallon retail.

Von Koolbergen was well known to Calgary police for his spy activities. Some 3 years previously, he had made himself notorious in the United States and western Canada in regard to spy plots and German espionage activities. While no incriminating evidence was found at the time, Von Koolbergen later is alleged to have said that he received $3,000 from German agents for information concerning Canadian military installations.

On September 3rd, 1918, Von Koolbergen and Charlie Pace received 6 months each under the Inland Revenue Act. It seemed that his "spy activities" had at least caught up with him in a roundabout way.

Large stills also appeared at Water Valley, north west of Calgary; at Acme, north east of Calgary; at St. Albert, north of Edmonton; and another just north of Lethbridge. These were all extensive operations requiring considerable equipment and a well organized system of disposing of the daily make. Many of the smaller operators, without adequate connections to dispose of their wares, were forced to cache their liquor and wait for buyers.

In Edmonton, a civic employee inadvertently stumbled onto a cache of 129 bottles of indifferent beer. In Calgary, two young boys playing golf on the Mount Royal course, hit a ball into a sand trap and while extricating it unearthed a cache of rye whiskey.

PRESSURE CREATES COUNTER PRESSURE

Almost from the beginning of prohibition, the story had been one of police pressure being applied and of counter measures being taken. A large faction of the citizens still favoured prohibition in 1918 and their most vocal spokesmen were the executive of the Social Service League. The League kept up a steady pressure on the government for more rigid laws and stricter enforcement. Opposition members likewise attacked the government over the failure of the A.P.P. to quash the movement of liquor in the province.

The Provincial Police, thinly spread, and engaged in the enforcement of **all laws**, had not the time to devote their complete energies to the suppression of the liquor traffic. Nevertheless, in the face of constant criticism and demand for action, they had to react, and unfortunately they began to resort more and more to questionable tactics.

25

The "Murchuk" case left a bitter taste in the mouths of the public.

Mike Murchuk, a petty thief in Calgary, had been arrested in a gambling raid in late April of 1918. Persuaded by members of the A.A.P. to act as a "spotter", Murchuk arranged to purchase a bottle of rye from Clerk Charles Foster at the St. Louis Hotel in Calgary, and then informed the police. Foster, together with Charles Smith, Joseph August and Mike Munson, was arrested in connection with the transactions.

At the trial, defense counsel, Mr. J. McKinley Cameron — who appeared on behalf of numerous citizens charged under the Act — drew from Murchuk the admission that he, Murchuk, was an alien, and that he wasn't above lying if the need arose. Deploring the fact that the police were resorting to the use of "alien stoolpigeons" instead of sticking to Canadian born informers, Mr. Cameron switched tables and had Murchuk charged with purchasing liquor illegally. Before the warrant could be procured and served, Murchuk disappeared from the courtroom and took his dubious talents elsewhere.

Another favorite trick of the harassed police was for two men from one detachment to go in plain clothes to another detachment, where they were unknown to the local bootlegging gentry, and on leads supplied by the home-town A.P.P. arrange to purchase liquor from the illegal vendors. This device, technically known as "entrapment", showed the desperate straits to which the police were driven by the never-ending light of criticism and demand for results. This, too, despite the assurances of the Premier on the floor of the Legislature, that the Attorney General's department would not permit the police to use this stratagem.

In the face of this increased pressure from the police, with whom they had lived in relative harmony to this point, the rum runners and illicit still owners began to apply counter-measures in the way of bribery, payoffs and "entrapment".

For example, at Lethbridge in mid-July of 1918, 15 cases of whiskey — the property of the R . . . gang of rum-runners — were cached on the farm of a man named Taylor at Coaldale. Two members of the A.P.P., Warman and Marion, arrived at the farm with two "special constables" and seized the liquor.

When Mr. Taylor did not receive a summons to appear in court, he went to the Lethbridge A.P.P. detachment to ask some discreet questions.

In the resulting investigation conducted by Superintendent Bryan, it transpired that the two "special constables" were Harold Rutledge and John Brown, both well known in the bootleg circles. While A.P.P. Constables Warman and Marion were each fined $75 and dismissed from the force, Rutledge and Brown had to be released when it was discovered that the liquor had been stolen from the place where they had cached it and that no "evidence" remained.

At Coutts, on the U.S. border, A.P.P. Constable A. E. Smith was reputed to have been offered $5,000 just to absent himself from his post for two days.

There is evidence that a good deal of money began to flow from the rum runners to various police and other government servants.

The struggle was not without its odd touch of humor.

While Detective Egan and Constable Wigs, A.P.P., were engaged on a hunt for stills in the Coalhurst area in September, 1918, a man walked up to them and asked them if they wanted to purchase a bottle of good whiskey. They followed him to an auto filled with booze which had just been brought in from Glasgow, Montana. The result was inevitable, but, on evidence supplied by the driver of the vehicle, charges were laid against a customs official at Coutts and a member of the A.A.P. who had conspired to pass the shipment through the customs point.

An ironic twist was added to the scene, which was rapidly becoming both bizzare and serious, when thieves broke into the Government Vendor store on 10th Avenue West in Calgary on the night of April 18th, 1919. Unable to break into the vaults where the bulk of stock was stored, the gang made off with between 500 and 600 bottles of liquor from the main room. They later learned that their "haul" consisted of bootleg booze which had been confiscated from stills and had been condemned as undrinkable!

In the face of tightening surveillance and harassment from the bedeviled police, the rum runners and bootleggers began to organize vertically. The proud owner of an illicit still began to hire his own transport drivers and to develop his own sources of outlet. The astute possessor of an "unwritten agreement" with a brewery or an export house did likewise. There is no evidence that any great amount of horizontal organization took place — that is, where bootleggers gathered together to distribute, or where transporters pooled their resources to freight the contraband. Quite the contrary, there is ample indication that each organization operated independently with their own special "protection" arrangements, and that considerable informing went on between the rival gangs. Only at the top level — the suppliers — does there appear to have been conspiracy and co-operation for mutual, increased benefits.

An example of the horizontal type of organization revolved around the operations of the large still situated near Acme, Alberta. Functioning with a capacity of some 125 gallons a day, the unknown operator of the still employed John Greeberg and Mike Segal to transport the produce to Calgary, Red Deer, Edmonton and other drought areas. At the city limits in each instance, the bottles, packed in gunny sacks, were transshipped from the new Chevrolets to less conspicuous means of transportation, such as wagons, buggies, drays, etc. The sacks were then delivered to a specific group of cafe owners, pool room proprietors and livery stables, who were part of the total set-up.

A prominent resident of Lacombe recalls his part in this chain as follows:

"I had instructions to leave my sleigh in back of the hotel at certain times. When I came out of the hotel I would hitch up and drive off. There was always a pile of rugs and blankets in back of the sleigh and I was advised not to look under these. Once I did, but all I saw was some milk cans and they sure weren't mine. I would drive the load up as far as Leduc and park behind the old Leland Hotel. When I came out in the morning, the milk cans would be gone and there would be $20 in an envelope stuffed under the front seat. Where the milk cans went from there, of course, I don't know. I suppose "they" had some other arrangement for getting them on up the line."

The products from this particular still near Acme were always identifiable by the labels on the bottles: "Peter Dawson". Police were confident that these labels were being forged at a printing plant in Calgary.

Although Greenberg and Segal were apprehended on more than one occasion and their loads and vehicles confiscated, no clue to the whereabouts of the large still was forthcoming and the plant continued in operation until the decline of Prohibition.

In the game of Pressure and Counter Pressure, the Honorable Mr. J. R. Boyle, Attorney General, announced in the Legislature on February 21st, 1919, that the A.P.P. would be re-organized to meet the new demands of total prohibition. The Police Commission, long a prime target of opposition members, was to be abolished and would be replaced by a single Commissioner of Police, who would be directly responsible to the Attorney General. Later, on March 3rd, Premier Charles Stewart gave more details. The enforcement of the Liquor Act would be taken out of the hands of the regular A.P.P. men and put under a specially created body of plain clothes detectives. Also, the liquor laws would be tightened up.

There were several areas of concern. Government vendors were complaining of the competition of the drug stores; the citizen who bought his "legal medicine" complained of the disparity in prices. Scotch at the Vendor's averaged $3.00 a quart, compared with $5.50 at the drug store. Rum was $3.50 at the Vendors — $7.00 over the druggist's counter. Worse still, the price of bootleg hooch had risen to $20.00 a gallon for beer and nearly $15.00 a bottle for hard liquors.

Probably the jump in illicit prices was caused by the increased amounts demanded for pay-offs.

The police were concerned officially with the loose methods of bookkeeping employed by the druggists. In fact, where the purchase and sale of liquor was concerned, most sets of books in the province were an auditor's nightmare.

Nor were the government vendors in any better shape. This fact was brought to light as a result of a sensational charge made by Mr. F. G. Forster, Provincial License Inspector until his retirement on November 7th, 1918. In a letter to the Hon. J. R. Boyle, Attorney General, Mr. Forster charged that Mr. Lucien Boudreau, M.L.A. for St. Albert, and incedently President of the Dominion Drug Company of Edmonton, had obtained $400 worth of liquor from the Edmonton vendor on credit. Since Mr. Boudreau was not privileged under the Act to purchase liquor, both the granting of credit and the actual removal of the liquor — if proven — would have been illegal.

In testimony taken before the Public Accounts Committee of the Legislature, both William J. Webster, the Edmonton Vendor, and Lucien Boudreau denied the charges. Evidence given by Mr. Forster and by a clerk in the vendor store affirmed the charges.

In an unprecedented secret session of the Committee on April 10th, 1919, the Committee members decided by a vote of 20-13 that Mr. Boudreau did not commit the offences alleged by Mr. Forster. On April 16th, after a long and heated debate in the Legislature, during which severe criticism was levelled at the Public Affairs Committee for resorting to secret session, Mr. Boudreau was finally cleared by a vote of 26-20 in his favour.

Most damaging of all the testimony given in the sordid affair was the admission by the Government Vendor that his bookkeeping system was "inadequate" and that he only checked his stock twice a year.

Another area of concern in the liquor trade was expressed by top officials of the A.P.P. that certain breweries were involved in "questionable decisions" regarding their shipments of liquor. On March 23rd, Detective E. T. Schoeppe and Constable Ruby had seized 10 bottles of "legitimate" beer at Olds; on March 27th, they had confiscated 10 barrels of beer shipped by the Edmonton Breweries to the Victoria Hotel in Olds; and two days later they had impounded 94 barrels of Cascade beer shipped by Vancouver breweries to Polar Aerated Water Company of Calgary; and all of these shipments had been tested from 4% to 6% over the legal percentage of alcoholic content allowable in "temperance beer".

More interesting was an allegation made by Chief Detective J. D. Nicholson. According to sleuth Nicholson, 25 barrels of beer shipped from Nat Bell warehouse in Edmonton, under the supervision of A.P.P. men, were found to be pure ice water when delivered to the consignee, Boivin Wilson & Co., of Montreal.

His accusation highlighted a long-standing suspicion that certain liquor concerns were shipping out water and recording the shipments on their inventory as liquor. The real liquor was then spirited out a side door for delivery to illicit sources. The exisience of such a subterfuge implied conspiracy between suppliers and consignees, as well as distributors.

NEW LEGISLATION

With so many areas of concern, with so many loopholes left unplugged, further restrictions were inevitable.

On March 3rd, 1919, another deputation from the Social Service League, headed by Rev. Mr. Coone, called on the Premier with a list of proposed amendments. The main recommendation was that in view of the demonstrated deplorable systems of bookkeeping currently in use by the legal dispensers of liquor, a new method of keeping track of the precious fluid was necessary. The League members proposed that consecutively numbered prescription pads should be issued to doctors and other privileged persons and that no orders for liquor might be filled by drug stores or vendors unless presented on one of these serialized forms. The forms would then be returned to the Attorney General's department at month end for verification.

In the amendments to the Liquor Act in 1919, this basic concept was adopted and all doctors were given a modest supply of these numbered prescription pads. They also provided that government vendors might sell on prescription, and, as a measure of relief to the "takers of medicine", the Act also decreed that the government would henceforth set the prices uniformly for both druggists and vendors.

The amendments pleased no one. The druggists complained that the 25% profit allowed them was too slender; the medical men viewed the serialized pads as a direct affront to their professional integrity. At their annual conventions, both professions suggested that the whole perscription business be taken out of their hands and be placed with the Attorney General's department.

In the beginning, the Attorney General undertook to dole out the prescription forms at the rate of 100 per week to each doctor. When one Edmonton physician used up his entire ration within a week and sent in for more, the Attorney General revised his "unwritten rule" and begun to issue only 150 each month to each doctor. Unused prescription forms were to be returned at the end of each month. The farcical nature of the whole business was that the Attorney General was literally forced into the position of "prescribing medicine without a license".

While the appearance of the numbered prescription pads assisted the bootleg trade, it did create a problem for those rascals who had been doing an excellent business in bogus prescriptions, and these were compelled to go into the counterfeiting business.

Within a short time, the government found itself in the position of having to issue a new series of pads almost every month. It was estimated that only 20 days elapsed between the issuance of a new series of prescription forms and the appearance of clever forgeries. The usual procedure was to photograph the new form, have a plate made, and then issue resembling duplicates. While the bulk of the counterfeiting was done in Montana, a bustling printing plant set up in the foothills north of Waterton, churned out bogus forms month after month. Each counterfeit brought from $1.00 to $3.00 on the illicit market.

The appearance of the new forms also brought about a rash of burglaries of doctors' offices across the land where the only items taken were the current supplies of legal prescription forms.

Also, because unused forms had to be returned at each month's end, there was a veritable parade to the doctor's office at the end of each month to see if there were any illnesses that might require a prescription on one of the remaining forms. It is safe to say that the bulk of the forms returned each month end to the Attorney General's office came from the druggists and vendors and not from doctor's offices.

Coincident with this effort to control the "medicine business", the government also revised its police force. The three-headed Police Commission was abolished and Alfred Cuddy, Calgary Police Chief, was appointed to the position of Commissioner on July 8th, 1919.

Born in County Tyrone, Ireland, in 1863, Alfred Cuddy had immigrated to Canada at the age of 19 and had joined the Toronto police force. Scarcely 12 months later, while on beat duty at the corner of Pearl and York streets, Cuddy came upon the scene just as "Blinky" Morgan, notorious Toronto hoodlum, gunned down an unarmed man named Maroney. Cuddy pursued Morgan, who fired at him and missed, and succeeded in disarming and arresting the desparado. He was promptly promoted to Constable First Class, and, after continued excellent service was shifted to the detective division. Among his achievements were the arrests of Dr. Holmes, whose wholesale insurance murders chilled the nation, and the rounding up and arrest of the "Dalton Imitators", a gang of misplaced western badmen who held up several jewellery stores and the Home Bank in Toronto. By 1906, he had risen to command the No. 2 Division in Toronto, which post he held until his resignation in 1912 to accept the post of Chief of Police in Calgary.

During service with the Calgary Police, his **piece-de-resistance** had been the tracking down and arrest of one of the "Exshaw murderers", who had shot down paymaster Wilson in the little mining town in mid-August, 1914.

He had once established a reputation for "putting on the lid", and he was said to have remarked that he could easily clean up illicit liquor in Calgary if given a free hand. With his appointment to the chief police post in the province, it appeared as if he was about to be given that opportunity, but on a much broader scale.

Since his appointment closely followed the declaration of Prohibition in the United States, which went into effect on July 1st, 1919, his tenure started under a seemingly lucky omen.

ALFRED CUDDY

THE GOOD NEIGHBOR POLICY

Prohibition in United States — more particularly in Montana and Utah — was a blessing for the rum runners. It was true that all three organizations in the south had prospered by running liquor from Montana into dry Alberta, but, with Montana also dry, their markets doubled. This time, the flow was from Fernie and the illicit stills in the mountains around the Pass southward. It was the good-neighbor policy in reverse.

During their early rum running days, all three men — Mr. R . . . in Lethbridge; Mr. Pick, at Blairmore, and Mr. Big in Fernie, had established excellent sources of supply in the neighboring states. These sources now proved useful as outlets.

Emilio Picariello, the Bottle King, branched out. Early in 1919, he purchased 2 McLaughlin Six Specials, one of the fastest cars on the road. So popular were these McLaughlins with the rum running fraternity that they were known as "Whiskey Sixes". Almost every owner of a McLaughlin, however innocent his reasons for acquiring one, was regarded with sly, knowing glances by his neighbors.

McLaughlin Buick

Mr. Pick's sources of supply were still based in Fernie, but there is indication that he drew upon the growing number of stills that were springing up in the mountains and along the back country trails. He also managed to import some strongly over-proof liquors from abroad, which when watered down to acceptable proportions brought excellent prices on the underground markets of Alberta and Montana.

Picking up his supplies at Fernie, or at the Alberta Hotel in Blairmore, Mr. Pick would make the run through the Pass, veer south near Pincher Creek across the almost trackless and fence-less foothills, and make his way through the Whiskey gap into the United States. He was often in competition with Mr. Big, from Fernie, who used the same basic route into Montana. In fact, the road from Fernie to Pincher Creek was know in police circles as "The Red Route", to distinguish it from the "Blue Route" which led from Coutts on the border, through Lethbridge and northward to Calgary and Edmonton.

On one of these trips through Whiskey Gap, Mr. Pick ran into a severe rainstorm which mired down his whiskey laden car. Going to a nearby house, he discovered two A.P.P. constables on patrol duty who had sought shelter from the storm. Enlisting their help to free his car from the mud, he waved a cheery goodbye, flashed his famous smile and drove on his way. The constables, never dreaming that the affable, farmerish-looking man in the sloppy blue-overalls was the noted "Emperor Pick", returned to the house to await the cessation of the storm so that they might resume their vigil for rum runners.

On another occasion, as Mr. Pick was returning from a trip into Montana, an American constable jumped on the running board just inside the border. The Emperor shot out his hand, fastened the constable in a vise-like grip and held him fast until the car had passed into Canadian territory.

There seems to have been an unwritten set of rules to the rum running game — rules which were followed by police in some in-stances and by the majority of "respectable" rum runners. One of these rules seems to have been that so long as the rum runner operated like a legitimate business man, they were not seriously molested. In this instance "legitimate" seemed to include owning one's own equipment, refraining from violence if accidently caught and refraining from stealing cars for transportation or theft of liquor from legal outlets. There is no indication that any of the three big operators in the south had their cars confiscated, while on the other hand, Albert Vaile and James Audette, who stole cars in their initial bids to break into the lucrative racket, received short shift from the police. Even Mr. Big, operating from Fernie, seems to have been almost immune.

It was common knowledge throughout the Pass that Emperor

Scene on The Red Route

Pick was in the rum running business and that as a profitable and necessary side-line he bought empty bottles. The Department of the Attorney General in Edmonton did an excellent business with The Bottle King in this latter respect and regularly sold The Emperor large shipments of empty beer and whiskey bottles. One recorded sale in May, 1919, was for 720 dozen bottles at 40 cents per dozen.

Meanwhile, hoping that Prohibition in Montana would assist in clearing up the mess, the A.P.P. under Commissioner Cuddy doubled their efforts to control the source of supply. Commissioner Cuddy made a flying trip to the trouble spot — the Crows Nest Pass — and a standard joke of the day was that every time he had a cup of coffee in a cafe, he sent part of the contents to the provincial analyst in Edmonton for inspection.

Together with Inland Revenue officers, the A.P.P. scoured the country for stills. A closer watch was kept on legal breweries who were still operating — though on greatly reduced bases — to produce the required amounts of "medicine" for local consumption. Pressure was increased on the pool halls, the cafes and the taverns that sold "temperance beverages". Despite the assurances of the Premier to the contrary, the A.P.P. men still approached doctors to try to purchase prescriptions, or druggists to fill them, or suspected bootleggers to try to purchase liquor. Often, they were successful, and 15 doctors were convicted in this manner in the space of one year.

The cutting off of the Montana and Utah supplies and the increased vigilance of the provincial and local police resulted in the creation of new stills and of a series of break-and-entries into drug stores from Regina to Edmonton. Apparently the work of one well-organized gang which took only liquor from the stores and operated upon a consistent pattern, the depradations began in July, 1919, and continued on well into the winter.

In addition to the well-known stills, whose locations still remained a secret but whose standard brands showed up regularly in raids on outlets, a number of smaller operations came and went. In 1919, 167 stills were seized. They were detected everywhere, from an unused Methodist church at Ranchville, Sask., to a stable in Drumhellar. One young Calgary lady recalls that her grandmother used to make beer in the kitchen while her policeman husband was out looking for moonshiners .

Stills were made of everything from wash boilers to Ford radiators. A special concoction, called "Squirrel Whiskey", appeared on the market. It had the kick of a cranky cow and retailed for $25.00 a quart. A humorous item in the **Macleod Times** for March 17th, 1923, reported that the police had at last discovered where the "kick" in Squirrel Whiskey came from. In a still that was raided

just north of Lethbridge, the A.P.P. men discovered two gophers, two mice, as well as a miscellaney of other articles in a pot of mash.

One of the most famous stills in the history of the Prohibition era — one that is fondly remembered by Calgarians even to this day — was located in the dignified confines of Calgary's Baptist Church. Caretaker Joe Salini conceived the idea of converting raisins into wine as a hobby to occupy himself when he wasn't keeping clean the pathway into Heaven and converted the organ loft into a modest manufacturing plant. While the good pastor marvelled at the way his congregation seemed to increase steadily, the local police were less charitable and on Friday, October 29th, they moved in and carted Joe and his equipment away. For the next six months, Joe devoted his janitorial talents to keeping the floors of the local pokey in spotless condition.

RETURN OF IMPORTATION

With Armistice on November 11th, 1918, there was an automatic 12 month period during which the ban against the intra-provincial transportation of liquor would remain in force. After that date, it would again be legal for exporters to ship across provincial borders. Eventually, January 1st, 1920, was chosen as the date upon which imports would again become legal. However, as early as October 7th, 1919, the Hon. C. J. Dorety introduced legislation into the House of Commons making it possible for any province, by means of a plebiscite, to prohibit importation into their province. In Alberta, the Social Service League made it known that they intended to press for such a plebiscite.

Nevertheless, as the year ended, the export liquor warehouses at Maple Creek, Golden, Fernie, Saskatoon and Regina re-opened their doors and began to lay in large stores, and, for the first time since 1917, the distilleries began to operate at full capacity. With unlimited importation, the A.P.P. men breathed a sigh of relief for they anticipated that both bootleggers and rum runners would be hard hit.

The exporters visualized no difficulty with transportation. Following the earlier debacle of 1917, when warehouses had been caught with large stocks on hand which the Dominion Express Company and the railroads had refused to accept for shipment, the warehouse owners had carried their cause to the courts, and it had been ruled that Express companies must accept shipments of liquor and the railways could not refuse to carry them. This judgement was still in effect.

Even on December 31st, the eve of "Der Tag", the moonshiners were still trying. Inspector Brankley and his men picked up

Samuel Graham and Carl Luchia at Langdon, where the latter had gone to pick up a load of hay consigned to them from Regina. Underneath the hay was an added attraction of $10,000 worth of bootleg rye.

The same night, Constable R. Wight, A.P.P., captured Jake Kruse with 25 gallons of moonshine just as Jake crossed the Red Deer river south of Drumhellar. When the total fine and costs came to $.196.00, Jake had to sell his team and wagon to raise the money. He realized $200 on the sale and, after paying the fine used the remaining $4.00 for train fare back to his still for another try at the big money.

In the south of the province, the Big Four merely shrugged their shoulders and hoped that the United States would not be so rash as to quash prohibition and put them out of business completely. At Lethbridge, Mr. R . . . and George F . . . modified their efforts slightly; Mr. Big in Fernie gave more attention to the southwest run; while Mr. Pick, at Blairmore celebrated the year end by distributing parcels of confections, fruit and beverages to the poor and by giving a free moving picture show to the school children of the town at the Opera House on Christmas Eve.

With the start of the new year, large orders were placed with export houses outside the province, all for small, legal-sized shipments to arrive daily, and the Express Companies began to set up separate quarters apart from their usual places of business to handle the anticipated flood. Special precautions were taken to guard against the pilfering from shed and storerooms that had marked the previous experience with export trade.

The price lists were eagerly awaited, and when they arrived, they were found to be most reasonable. Most hard liquors averaged $3.25 a quart, plus express charges, and while these were slightly higher than the drug store and vendor prices, they were far below the exhorbitant black-market prices.

Even before the first shipments arrived, the Social Service League was organizing for another campaign for intensified restrictions on the trade, but, in view of the proposed plebiscite on importation, the government held firm and left the Liquor Act unchanged. Instead, it turned its attentions to the Liquor Warehouse Act. In a surprise move, the government issued an ultimatum to the liquor warehouses to dispose of all stock before May 10th, 1920. After that date, all liquor on the premises would be removed to government supervised warehouses where it would be sold and the companies re-imbursed in this manner. However, because of difficulty in disposing of stocks, several extensions had to be granted, but, at the close of business on June 5th, A.P.P. men moved into export houses across the province and padlocked the doors. Since there was too much liquor on hand to be stored in the government vendors' warehouses, it had to be left under A.P.P. guard.

x Illustrating how Basset appeared when shooting Bailey dead. Bailey was unharmed in the building.

BELLEVUE CAFE

40

Even before the enforced closure, the export companies, spearheaded by the Gold Seal Liquor Company of Calgary, were contesting the issue in court. On Friday, July 2nd, 1920, the Appellate Division of the Supreme Court, with Justice Hyndman, Beck and Ives all agreeing, found that the government legislation was **ultra vires** and that the export companies could resume business. The keys to the warehouses were returned to the managers on the morning of July 6th.

Thwarted in their efforts to stamp out the export trade by direct legislation, the government issued a series of regulations on July 19th which gave them greater powers of inspection over the premises occupied by these concerns and imposed stricter inventory controls. These measures were clearly recognized as "stop gap", however, for October 25th, 1920, had been set as the date for holding the plebiscite on imports and the government anticipated that the decision of the electorate would be favorable.

With reports of prohibition violence in the United States an almost daily feature of the press, the people of Alberta had been wont to look upon their own untroubled waters with an air of smug righteousness. Suddenly, on August 2nd, 1920, the province was rudely startled.

It was 5:15 p.m., August 2nd, when one of the bloodiest dramas in the history of the Crows Nest Pass began. C.P.R. train No. 63, from Lethbridge to Cranbrook, was just nearing Sentinel way station when three unmasked men, Tom Basoff, George Arkoff, and Ausby Holloff (alias Aulcoff) who were travelling on the train, held the other passengers at gunpoint while they relieved them of their watches and wallets. It was said that they were after Emperor Pick, who was rumored to be carrying a roll of $10,000. In the confusion, Mr. Pick secreted his roll behind seat cushions and moved to a seat across the aisle. After collecting some $400 in cash and several watches, the men left the train and headed in the direction of Coleman.

A manhunt was immediately organized and A.P.P. men and R.C.M.P. constables were brought in from surrounding detachments. The trio turned up in Coleman on Friday, four days after the holdup, and not agreeing on the best method of escape, split up, with Aulcoff going into the United States while Bassoff and Arkoff headed east.

Bassoff and Arkoff arrived in Bellevue the following morning, Saturday, August 7th, and stopped at the Bellevue Cafe (now Jim's Cafe) for breakfast. Mr. Robertson, a local J.P., recognized Bassoff and called Constable James Frewin, of the A.P.P. at Blairmore. Frewin boarded a passing train and was on the scene in minutes.

Frewin was joined by Constable Ernest Usher, R.C.M.P., and Constable Fred Bailey, A.P.P., and the three entered the cafe by different doors. Frewin, who was understandable nervous, approached Bassoff and Arkoff at their booth and ordered the pair to put their hands up. As Bassoff was putting his coffee down, Frewin fired at him but missed. A tussle began and in the confusion both Arkoff and Bassoff got their guns from their coats and opened fire on the three policemen.

What happened inside the cafe is not known, but all managed to stumble outside, with both Arkoff and Const. Usher collapsing to their deaths. Tom Bassoff, who was wounded in the leg, killed Bailey in the doorway and hobbled off down the street in the direction of the Frank Slide.

The posse converged on Bellevue and searched for five days around the slide area and neighboring towns. During the search, Constable Hidson, who was going through deserted houses, accidently shot Special Constable Nick Kysli, thinking he was Bassoff. This brought the total deaths to four.

Bassoff was picked up Wednesday night, August 11th, near a hayshed at Pincher Creek as he was eating. He was tried at Lethbridge on October 12th, 1920, was convicted of murder and finally executed on December 22nd, 1920. His was the fifth death.

Ausby Aulcoff was not found until 1924, in Butte, Montana. He was returned to Canada for trial and on January 26th, 1924, was sentenced to 7 years in the peniteniary. He died there of natural causes a few years later.

Police officers called in for this manhunt from outside detachments felt that more serious trouble in this area was very near the surface. Said one: "The operations of the army of whiskey peddlers in every Pass town is rapidly becoming a menace, but the police officers stationed there are entirely insufficient to stamp out the traffic. Fortunes are being made . . . They work, unmolested, at all hours. There is nothing underhand with these men and they sell just as openly as in the days before prohibition made its entry into Alberta. Whiskey by the glass or bottle can be purchased openly and without fear of interruption. All that is needed is the 50 cents for each drink."

Local gossip in the Pass indicated that the problem was even more serious. There were ugly rumors that some local police were involved and that payoffs were being made. Mr. Pick made regular payments to a high government official. On one occasion, having delivered his payment to the prominent resident of Blairmore who was the go-between, Mr. Pick and his wife watched the man board the local train. Following the train to Calgary by auto, Mr. Pick tailed the go-between to an office near the C.P.R. station. While he waited discreetly outside until he was sure that the money had changed hands, Pick then walked into the office. After being introduced to the flustered official as: "The man who is paying you the money," Picariello shook hands and left. "I just wanted to see where my money was going," he later explained.

When it was considered that the bulk of the population in southern Alberta was still "wet" in their drinking philosophy, the difficulty of policing the area assumed its proper proportion — it was impossible. And if the occasional policeman, influenced by public pressure, relaxed his efforts to stamp out the popular traffic, it was understandable. When Emilio Picariello's safe was opened after his death, it was found to contain numerous notes from police officials in the Pass giving the dates of upcoming weddings, reunions and other celebrations, together with suggestions as to the beverages that might make the occasions more spirited. In an age when almost every able-bodied man carried a concealed weapon and when these men were determined to drink at any cost, no one wished to apply too much pressure. The Bellevue Cafe murders were an example of what could happen.

Keenly aware of this trend in thinking in southern Alberta, the Social Service League, which was gearing up for a propaganda assault on the electorate preparatory to the holding of the October 25th plebiscite, appointed an organizer for Calgary, one for Edmonton, but none for the south.

When the plebiscite was held and the final vote was tabulated, the over-all majority in favor of more prohibition was 18,993, but there were some sobbering figures. The south voted strongly for importation. In Calgary, with a total of 13,069 votes cast, the importation issue was defeated by a scant majority of only 699. Edmonton and the central portions of the province (where rum running and bootlegging were relatively minor evils) gave prohibition its deciding majority.

The final date set for the cessation of importation was February 1st, 1921.

RISING OPPOSITION

As the government prepared for its important 1921 legislative session, it became apparent that there were two bodies of opinion already shaping up. There had been a growing feeling in the government circles that full control of liquor distribution should be taken over by the government and handled through the vendors, rather than continuation of the sale through prescription and drug stores. Attorney General Boyle repeatedly pointed out the difficulties of trying to stem the traffic when almost half the people favored drinking. Another disturbing factor was that British Columbia had recently returned to a "wet" state. Fortunately for the rum runners, and unfortunately for the police, both Saskatchewan and Montana were still dry.

The other faction in the cabinet was in favour of hiring more policemen to enforce the existing legislation.

These two views were echoed in the community by the ever-vigilant Social Service League, whose aims were well known, and by the mergence of a new and vocal group who called themselves the Moderation League of Alberta. Under the strong leadership of William Short, K. C., the Moderates were campaigning for a new Act to provide for the open sale of liquor under government control. Even such staunch supporters as Bob "Calgary Eye Opener" Edwards, who had initially supported prohibition (though a drinking man himself) were beginning to wonder openly as to the wisdom of continuing to deny the citizen his "pint".

On July 18th, 1921, the government of Charles Stewart was soundly defeated at the polls by the United Farmers Party under Herbert Greenfield, and the task of trying to enforce a law with nearly one half the people against him fell to Attorney General J. E. Brownlee. However, despite the change of government, no changes in the situation were made in 1921. Importation was still banned and the province returned to bootlegging, moonshining and rum running. The average citizen, otherwise quite law-abiding, was forced to return to deceit and trickery in order to obtain "a pint of the best", only to discover all too often that it was pretty vile stuff.

The illicit liquor traffic increased in volume and intensity. A new breed of rum runner seemed to be moving into the picture. Break-ins at government vendor stores increased; freight trains in transit were looted of valuable cargos on the move; illicit stills sprang up — a fresh one every day — in addition to the old standbys which flourished anew. A.P.P. men declared that there were bootleggers and stills in every city, town and village in the province.

The new rum runners, James Audette, Graham Duncan, Albert Vaile and William Armston, to mention a few, seemed to prefer to steal cars rather than invest in their own equipment. These activities were frowned upon by both police and respectable rum runners.

In the regular reports sent in by A.P.P. officers in charge of liquor squads, new names were constantly being added to the old stand-bys. In a secret report forwarded by Detective Lawrence to the officer commanding "D" Division, Lethbridge, 8 minor rum runners were listed, together with the make of their cars, the license number and the serial numbers — that is, 8 in addition to the 2 big operators, Mr. R . . . and George F . . . .

Mr. Big, of Fernie, continued to run quietly and unobtrusively down through Elko and across Tobacco Plains into Utah via Roosville, but he was getting competition.

"Buck Tooth" McCarty, of Eureka, Montana, and Oscar Bjork did a lively business with their Oldsmobile, which could carry 10 cases. The picturesque Howard W. Brown, of Roosville, who described himself as a "common carrier" for police records, carried on a prosperous business.

But, the big man of the Pass was still the popular and smiling Emilio Picariello. Despite a rash of small, fly-by-night operators who rose and fell in their efforts to de-throne him, Mr. Pick replaced his McLaughlin Sixes with McLaughlin Sevens and continued to carry on business from the old stand. His durability helped to reassure the jittery patrons. A member of the Blairmore Town Council, he continued to earn the respect of his fellowmen by acts of generosity. During the 1918 miner's strike, he contributed handsomely to the families of the men out of work; at Christmas time he purchased whole carloads of flour to be distributed to the poor in Blairmore and his home town of fond memories — Fernie.

As a mark of his respectability, the local newspaper refrained from publishing his name when it discussed the monthly meetings of the bootleg fraternity.

THE ALBERTA HOTEL

45

From time to time, Mr. Pick made minor contributions to provincial coffers.

Early in the spring of 1921, A.P.P. officers under the direction of Sgt. J. J. Nicholson — acting on an anonymous tip — raided the Emperor's warehouse and decided that its contents were contraband and would have to be confiscated. They carted off 213 barrels to be stored in the old Frank Sanatorium building. Samples from some of the barrels were sent to Edmonton for analysis and it was found that 4 of these contained liquor which was slightly over the legal percentage. The other 9 were "temperance beer" strength.

After innumerable delays, the case finally came to court on June 10th, and Mr. Pick was fined $20 and costs and suffered the loss of 4 barrels out of the 213. The rest were carted back to his warehouse in the basement of the hotel. Considering the court's time, the legal expenses of prosecution, and the transportation of the barrels to and from Pick's hotel, the amount of the fine seemed to fall considerably short of the expense of collecting it.

In efforts to tighten police control, Attorney General Brownlee placed Detective E. T. Schoeppe in charge of operations in the south and moved Sgt. J. J. Nicholson from Blairmore to Edmonton, where he was placed in charge of enforcing the Liquor Act throughout the province. It was felt that his experience gained in the rough and tumble atmosphere of the Pass would be invaluable in other areas of the province.

In April, 1922, Commissioner Alfred Cuddy announced his resignation, effective June 15th, to accept the position of Assistant Commissioner of the Ontario Provincial Police. His had not been a happy tenure. Hampered by lack of funds and personnel, at times hopelessly ham-strung by events outside his department, and being continually in the limelight of criticism, Cuddy, like his predecessors and those who would follow, had made little or no headway against the insidious flow of illegal liquor. His place was taken by W. C. Bryan, Superintendent, and his offices of Commissioner and Superintendent were combined.

By the spring of 1922, the government of Mr. Greenfield was definitely swinging towards fuller governmental control of the liquor business. In a rapid series of amendments, the government opened dispensaries in new centers and confined the drug stores to dispensing "medicine" in 6 ounce bottles instead of the usual 40 ounce size. An additional 50 men were added to the A.P.P., and Mr. E. S. Bishop was appointed to be a Commissioner under the Liquor Act. Mr. Bishop was to have control of the administative functions, while Sgt. J. J. Nicholson remained in charge of the police activities.

One of the new members added to the A.P.P. in its efforts to suppress the liquor traffic was Stephen O. Lawson. Borne at

46

Brixton, Surry, England, on June 8th, 1880, Steve Lawson came to Canada in 1903 and west in the spring of 1904. After ranching in the Macleod district for 3 years, he joined the Macleod police on May, 7th, 1907, and rose to become Chief of Police. At the outbreak of war, he enlisted and served overseas. On his discharge, he became Police Chief of Fernie in 1920 and served with that force until his enlistment in the A.P.P. on March 12th, 1922. He was then stationed at Coleman, a little mining town west of Blairmore that straddled the main highway used by the rum runners.

His counterpart in Coleman was Police Chief James Houghton, head of the local one-man police force. His function was primarily to serve as a look-out man for convoys of rum runners passing through his territory.

On September 21st, 1922, Constable R. M. Day, A.P.P., at Blairmore, received information from a stool-pigeon that Mr. Pick was going to Fernie for a load of liquor. The word was passed to the look-out post at Coleman, and Lawson and Houghton maintained a vigilance from 10 to 4 p.m. Later, a message was received from Fernie — source unknown — that Mr. Pick was returning with his load.

About 4 o'clock, Steve Lawson and Chief Houghton watched as the little cavalcade of rum runners proceeded down the main street of Coleman (there was no side road). The first McLaughlin was driven by J. J. McAlpine, the Emperor's mechanic; and the second was handled by Steve Picariello, 19; and the last McLaughlin Seven was piloted by the Bottle King himself. Neither policeman made any effort to stop the cars — this was not their job — and Constable Lawson merely reported the progress of the cars by phone to Sergeant James Scott, at Blairmore, who was in charge of the district.

Allowing sufficient time for the cars to reach the Alberta Hotel, Sgt. Scott went to the Hotel with Const. Day. Finding Emilio Picariello outside the hotel, Scott served him with a search warrant and advised him that they had come for the contraband load. Pick dashed to his car and signalled on the horn. The police rushed to the rear of the building in time to see young Steve roar off in a McLaughlin, and, securing their own police vehicle, they took off in pursuit. By this time, Mr. Pick was already underway, protecting the rear of his son's vehicle. At one point, Sgt. Scott took to the ditch and managed to pass the Emperor's car, but, when he slowed down at the Greenhill Hotel to allow Constable Day to get to a phone and alert the police at Coleman, Picariello, Sr., passed him, and by skillful jockeying prevented the police car from overtaking the fleeing McLaughlin.

About a mile from Blairmore, Scott abandonned the chase.

Travelling at speeds between 40 and 50 miles an hour, Steve

Picariello raced for the B.C. border, while his father, the immediate danger passed, followed at a more leisurely pace.

At Coleman, warned by Chief Houghton that the cars were returning, Constable Lawson stepped to the middle of the street in an attempt to halt the boy. When Steve refused to stop, Lawson fired at him twice, wounding him in the hand. Commandeering the car of William Bell, a local resident, Lawson and Houghton gave chase and fired a third shot at the speeding McLaughlin before the police car suffered a flat and had to pull up. Steve Picariello disappeared in a cloud of dust in the direction of Michel.

On the return trip to Coleman, the policemen met Mr. Pick, and Constable Lawson stopped to speak to him. "You might as well bring the boy back, for if you don't, I will," Lawson advised. The matter was left at that, with no threats on either side. Mr. Pick continued on towards Crows Nest, a small village on the border, to get news of his son and his load, while Lawson and Houghton returned to Coleman.

At Crows Nest, Mr. Pick evidently learned that the police the police had shot his son, but there was no indication of the severity of the injury. It was known, however, that the boy was still alive.

On his return to Blairmore, Emperor Pick overtook Sgt. Scott and talked good-naturedly with the police officer. According to Scott's later testimony, Pick said: "So, you didn't get the load." Scott replied that he wasn't finished. There would be charges under the Motor Vehicle Act. Pick is said to have replied: "I saved my load, anyway, and I don't care how many times I ditch you. It was lucky for Lawson that he did not kill my boy, or else I would kill him."

Later that evening, learning that his son had been arrested and was being held prisoner, Emilio decided to go to Coleman and confront Lawson. Florence Lassandro, 22-year-old wife of his close associate Charles Lassandro, insisted on accompanying him. Borrowing a McLaughlin owned by Andrew Petrie, which had been left with mechanic McAlpine for overhaul, he drove the short 4 miles to Coleman and stopped in front of the police barracks. Steve Lawson came over to the car and stood with one foot on the running board while they talked.

According to Mrs. Lassandro, who was the only person to make a statement later, Pick said: "You shot my boy and you're going with me to get him." Lawson said that he did not know where the boy was. Pick insisted and an argument followed when Lawson refused to accompany them. During the heat of the argument, Emilio seized his gun in order to enforce his command. Lawson grappled with him and in the struggle the gun exploded several times — one shot ripped through the dashboard and others shattering the windshield.

48

In a moment of panic, as the shots were flying and she saw the gun muzzle swing towards her, Mrs. Lassandro fired at the constable, who had both arms around Picariello's neck. The bullet entered Lawson's shoulder at the back and traversed his body as he was leaning on the car. He staggered back and fell to the ground just as the McLaughlin roared away. Within a few minutes he was dead.

Emilio Picariello was arrested in Blairmore the following day and Florence Lassandro gave herself up to the police later in the afternoon. Both were charged with murder, though it is difficult in the light of history to believe that either Emilio Picariello or Mrs. Lassandro had gone to Coleman with the intention of killing the police officer. Their actions, and the actions of Steve Lawson, which took place within the vision of several eye witnesses, seem to bear out Mrs. Lassandro's contention that Pick unreasonably insisted that Lawson accompany them to find Steve Picariello; that when the officer refused, Pick threatened him with the gun; and that Lawson grappled courageously with him and Mrs. Lassandro fired in fear and panic.

Even at this hour, Emilio Picariello could not escape the contact with liquor which seemed to shadow his entire career in the Pass.

A.P.P. Barracks, Coleman

49

A Case of "Pickled Pork"

The Cadillac which drove him from Blairmore to the provincial jail at Lethbridge was owned and driven by a Mr. Mark Rogers, a wholesale liquor dealer from Lethbridge.

There followed a long series of trial and appeals following the conviction, but finally the last appeal was refused and Emilio and the young girl were executed at Fort Saskatchewan jail on the morning of May 3rd, 1923. Undoubtedly, had the fervor of Prohibition been missing, both would have and should even then have received commutations.

Even as the shocked province followed the inevitable sequence of inquest, preliminary, trial and appeals which followed the fatal shooting, the rum runners and the bootleggers carried on their trades.

In a survey of liquor conditions issued by the government at the end of 1922, it was estimated that approximately 10% of the 260 drug stores in the province were violating the Act; 40% of the 414 pool halls seemed to be engaged in the trade; and some 30% of the 2002 cafes were problem spots. An outstanding example of the latter was Charlie Hon of the City Cafe in Brant. Charlie used to pass drinks across the counter with the abandon of a man selling ice cream cones on a hot August afternoon. After several convictions, the Attorney General suspended Charlie's license and Charlie left for parts unknown, abandoning $1,000 bail money as his contribution to the provincial coffers.

Illicit stills continued to pour out quantities of indifferent liquor in a steady stream. Editor Charles Clark, of the **High River Times**, after citing two incidents where residents of High River had come upon large caches of liquor, commented: "High River must be a gold mine of caches if they can be stumbled upon by innocents so easily, which leads us to wonder if all the other towns and villages in the province are equally favored with these natural resources."

Veteran A.P.P. officers could have assured him that High River was not the only blessed place.

With increased vigilance on the part of the liquor squad, greater precautions were taken by the bootlegging fraternity to conceal their produce, but possibly the most novel method of all was displayed by Alex Ballenger, a one-legged Spartonberg Negro. Alex used his hollowed-out leg to transport his wares, but his downfall came when he walked past a policeman who became curious about the stealthy "sloosh". Alex was fined $100 for transporting liquor.

But, even as Emilio Picariello and Florence Lassandro waited out their last days in the prison at Fort Saskatchewan, a movement was underway to kill prohibition in the province. During the late fall and early winter of 1922, a petition was circulated by the Hotelmen's Association, praying for government control of the liquor trade and the return of licensed parlours and bars. It is entirely possible that many persons, appalled by the tragedy and the violence that seemed to accompany all efforts to enforce Prohibition, both in the United States and Canada, willingly signed the petition in order to prevent more disorder and law breaking . . .

And, more violence was promised in a proud display of new equipment by the Alberta Provincial Police designed to meet the liquor traffic problems anticipated during the summer of 1923. In the display were six powerful motorcycles, two of which were mounted with machine guns that were aimed by steering the bike. Standard equipment on the other four were sidecars and submachine guns.

When finally presented to the government in January 1923, the Hotelmen's Association petition contained 51,000 names. The Hon. Vernon W. Smith, Minister of Railways & Telephones, was appointed chairman of a special committee to investigate the validity of the petition, and on March 8th, he reported back to the Premier that the petition was in order.

Despite the protests of a delegation of more than 200 members of the Social Service League who called on Premier Greenfield the following day, the Premier ordered holding of a third plebiscite, to take place on Monday, November 5th, 1923.

The machinery for holding the referendum under the Direct Legislation Act was set in motion.

Even as the people were moving towards their third crucial decision, new evidence was being presented to uphold the view that prohibition was a greater evil than the ills it sought to cure.

On the night of May 2nd, even as Emilio Picariello and Florence Lassandro were spending their last hours in their death cells, another man died because of the liquor traffic.

At Drumhellar, at about 10:30 in the evening, Chief of Police Fletcher and Constable Charles M. Paris attempted to stop a high-powered McLaughlin roadster piloted by 33 year old Elmo E. Trider, and loaded with 9 sacks of liquor, each containing about 12 bottles. Mounting the running board, the policemen attempted to stop the vehicle by shooting at the front tires, but failed. A few moments later, as the driver attempted to negotiate a sharp turn near the railway, the roadster went out of control and smashed into a wooden fence.

Constable Paris was killed instantly.

Charged with murder, Trider was finally acquitted by a jury on June 2nd, but was fined $200 and costs under the Liquor Act.

Even though the handwriting seemed clear on the whiskey bottle label, local moonshiners were still hoping.

On the afternoon of May 11th, 1923, Calgary City Police received a tip that a large still was located in a prominent residence in Mount Royal. The local Inland Revenue office was contacted and a raiding party was organized under James Dalgetty, of that department, and Det. Sgt. Yeats, of the city police.

As they appproched the house at 2917 - 8th Street West, perched on a hill overlooking the peaceful Mount Royal Golf Course and Elbow Park, the raiding party began to suspect that "they had been given a bum steer". The houses was well-lighted, a water sprinkler played over the neatly manicured lawn. Everything was homelike, including the chatter of children being put to bed. Nevertheless, they persisfed. Finding a chink of light from a basement window, they peered through and beheld a cellar almost completely filled with moonshine equipment A man and youth were even intent upon sampling their latest batch.

When the officers entered and seized the equipment, they were astounded at the efficiency of the operation. By far the largest still ever seized in the province, the plant occupied the whole basement, except for a space for the furnace. There were 12 barrels of mash merrily fermenting away, and about 70 gallons of excellent Scotch whiskey ready for shipment. The equipment included two stills, a purifying device, a miniature bottling plant, as well as quantities of labels, bottles and corks.

Mr. George Packwood, owner of the display, remarked as he and his son were led away: "Yes, I voted for prohibition, and I'd vote for it again. I went broke farming."

When November 5th rolled around and the vote was tabulated, the majority in favour of taking the liquor out of the hands of bootleggers and rum runners and placing distribution in the hands of the government was 32,210.

In compliance with the wishes of the majority, the government proceeded to draw up amendments to the Liquor Act which would provide for the establishment of an Alberta Liquor Control Board, the re-admission of liquor for consumption in private residences, in bonafide clubs for members only, and in parlours in those places where special premises had been set aside from the dining area. Missing from the Act as originally passed were such present-day refinements as permitting liquor to be consumed in restaurants or dining rooms, or any provision for men and women to drink together in the same room.

On May 10th, 1924, by proclamation of the Alberta Liquor Act, prohibition in Alberta came to an end.

Gradually the illicit stills fell into decay; the bootlegger became a "small potato man" who merely supplemented some legitimate income by supplying the odd bottle to customers who became thirsty in the middle of the night; and the old time rum runners counted

53

their bank accounts and retired gracefully. For a while, fly-by-night runners played the American market of Montana, but conditions were changed. It was no longer considered respectable, even in the Pass, to be engaged "in the trade", and these die-hards — lacking the protection of the people — quickly fell prey to police patrols.

Today, the ghostly Whiskey Sixes no longer whisk along the dusty highways of Alberta or slink across the fenceless prairie in order to avoid police barricade; the men who drove them have scattered — although a certain bartender still gets a twinkle in his eye as he recalls the time he drove a McLaughlin Buick over an embankment at 100 miles an hour to avoid a road block — but almost every old-timer from Coutts to St. Paul has a story to relate (always about somebody else) about "the business".

Here and there is a relic of the past: The Fernie Dairy occupies the building which once supplied so much liquor for the parched throats of Alberta, Montana and Utah; a modest monument in Water Valley marks the site of the old whiskey still there; and there are still some of Mr. Pick's famous 40 ounce bottles around.

It is true that today the occasional "village drunk" is seen in certain parts of Calgary, Lethbridge and Edmonton, but this seems a small price to pay in contrast with the tension, the ever-present threat of violence, and the indignity that the average citizen was once forced to endure in order to obtain "the jug of wine" that has traditionally gone along with "the loaf of bread, and Thou".

REFERENCES

Because of the confidential nature of most of the material included in this Frontier Book, the author can only thank those old-timers who reminisced with him and suggested slyly: "Why don't you go down to see . . . . He can tell you lots more about the trade." For these invaluable leads, my deep appreciation, Old Timers.

Frank W. Anderson, B.A., M.S.W.

THE FRONTIER SERIES

1. **THE FRANK SLIDE STORY:** On April 29, 1903, a 100-million-ton wall of rock split off Turtle Mountain and thundered toward the Crowsnest town of Frank. One hundred seconds later quietness returned — but seventy men, women and children were dead.

2. **MURDER ON THE PLAINS:** This collection of Western Canada's dramatic crimes includes an account of Swift Runner, who disposed of the evidence by eating his victims.

3. **THE RIEL REBELLION 1885:** Under the leadership of Louis Riel, dissatisfied Metis in Western Canada submitted a Bill of Rights to Ottawa, requesting permission to establish their own province. The results were tragic, and included death to many of the participants.

4. **THE LOST LEMON MINE:** All that is known about an 1870s gold discovery in the Rocky Mountains which created an Alberta legend and still fascinates treasure hunters.

5. **THE DYNAMIC CROWSNEST:** From the discovery of gold on Studhorse Creek in 1863 to threatened Indian warfare in the 1880s, from the rum-running days of the 1920s, until the present, this southernmost of the Rocky Mountain passes has been a route rich in history.

6. **EXPLORING SOUTHERN ALBERTA'S CHINOOK COUNTRY:** From the Rocky Mountains to the Cypress Hills, from the Drumheller badlands to the sparkling beauty of the 160-mile-long Kananaskis Forestry Trunk Road — in all over 90,000 square miles.

7. **Bill Miner TRAIN ROBBER:** Probably North America's greatest stagecoach and train robber, this quiet spoken man stole some $250,000 in a lifetime of crime. Included was $7,000 in 1904 from British Columbia's first train hold-up.

8. **INCREDIBLE ROGERS PASS:** In this 55-mile section of the Trans-Canada Highway over 200 men died keeping the CPR's mainline open and today snowsheds and artillery protect motorists from snowfall which can exceed 700 inches a year.

9. **REGINA'S TERRIBLE TORNADO:** On June 30, 1911, a tornado funneled into Saskatchewan's capital, transforming a quiet summer's day into one of destruction and death.

10. **BANFF — PARK OF ALL SEASONS:** A 15-square-mile reserve established around a Rocky Mountain hotsprings in 1885 developed into Banff National Park. Today Banff covers over 3,500 square miles and hosts over three million visitors a year.

11. **THE RUM RUNNERS:** During Alberta's 1916-24 prohibition era most citizens were determined to have their booze; others were willing to bring it to them. The price was high, with three Alberta policemen among those who died.

12. **THE HOPE SLIDE — Disaster in the Dark:** In the darkness of January 9, 1965, 100 million tons of rock buried B.C.'s Southern Trans-Provincial Highway over 100 feet in rocks, trees and mud, engulfing motorists already trapped by a snow slide.

13. **THE FRASER CANYON:** "We had to pass where no human beings should venture...." wrote Simon Fraser in 1808. In 1861-65 a road through the canyon to Barkerville cost $1 million — for 400 miles. Today's highway in places cost $2 million and more — a mile.

14. **Gabriel Dumont FRONTIERSMAN:** A superb horseman, marksman and natural leader, in the 1850s he fought the fierce Blackfoot and Sioux Indians on the prairie and later commanded Riel's forces during the Riel Rebellion.

15. **WATERTON NATIONAL PARK:** The Indians knew it as "Land of the Shining Mountains," a unique area in southwestern Alberta where prairie meets the mountains, where nature sculpted a chain of lakes and glacial valleys against a snow-peaked background.

16. **Death of Albert Johnson — THE MAD TRAPPER OF RAT RIVER:** One intriguing mystery remains in this saga of pursuit and shoot-out in Canada's Arctic nearly a half century ago — who was Albert Johnson?

17. **CALGARY-BANFF HIGHWAY:** The first indistinct link between what is now Calgary and Banff was forged in the early 1860s by fifteen lost miners. From this unpromising beginning evolved today's four-lane superhighway.

18. **HILLCREST MINE DISASTER:** Hillcrest Mine in Alberta's Crowsnest Pass was considered the safest in the region until a tragic June 19, 1914. That morning 235 men went into the miles of tunnels — moments later 189 died.

19. **THE DEWDNEY TRAIL — Hope to Rock Creek:** During the 1858 gold rush to what is today B.C., 25,000 miners stampeded north from California, threatening to make the region U.S. territory. The historic Dewdney Trail helped keep the area Canadian.

20. **THE DEWDNEY TRAIL — Rock Creek to Salmo:** More historical background on a trail which is today paralleled by B.C.'s Southern Trans-Provincial Highway 3.

21. THE DEWDNEY TRAIL — Salmo to Wild Horse Creek: In 1865 Dewdney's Trail was complete, 360 miles from the Fraser River to the Rockies.

22. THE CYPRESS HILLS OF ALBERTA-SASKATCHEWAN: Twenty miles wide, 200 miles long, nearly 5,000 feet high, they are a unique landform — ranking with the Grand Canyon and the desert of Western America.

23. The Calgary Stampede's HALF MILE OF HELL: The Stampede's popular chuckwagon race is nearly fifty years old, an exciting, fiercely competitive event that requires superb horsemanship and in which a fraction of a second can decide the winner.

24. CALGARY TO MEDICINE HAT: Highway history along some 180 miles of the Trans-Canada Highway across the prairies through country famous for pheasant, antelope, and irrigation, with access to the Drumheller badlands and 70-million-year-old dinosaur relics.

25. ALMIGHTY VOICE: Between 1895-97 one of the most dramatic manhunts in the Canadian West resulted in seven people shot dead, including three policemen.

26. OUTLAWS OF MANITOBA: They were hardened men who resisted arrest, tried to escape before being tried, and broke out of jails, ready to kill anyone who tried to stop them.

27. SERGEANT HARRY MORREN, RNWMP: In 3½ years Harry Fuller Morren, Royal North West Mounted Police, was involved in more dramatic episodes, including shoot-outs, than the average police officer in forty years.

28. SASKATCHEWAN PROVINCIAL POLICE: Despite popular legend, policing Western Canada was not restricted to the North West Mounted Police. From 1917-28 Saskatchewan had its own police force. Here is a look at some of its exploits.

29. THE CALGARY-EDMONTON TRAIL: Today it is a superhighway linking Edmonton and Calgary but its history, which includes outlaws, stagecoaches and cowboys, goes back nearly a century to the days when Calgary had a permanent population of thirty.

30. MAJESTIC JASPER: Massive mountains such as Edith Cavell; Miette Hot Springs and Maligne Lake; wildlife from moose to mountain sheep; and year-round activities from skiing to hiking, attract nearly two million people yearly to this largest of western national parks.

31. RIEL'S MANITOBA UPRISING: The story of Louis Riel is that of the Metis — a proud people who fought for the right to govern themselves as a province.

32. THE FROG LAKE MASSACRE: On April 17, 1885, telegraph wires across Canada carried a message from what is today Alberta: "There's been a massacre at Frog Lake. All the white men have been murdered and their wives taken prisoner by Big Bear's Plains Crees."

33. STOPS OF INTEREST IN ALBERTA Volume One: Along Alberta's highways are a series of excellent historical markers. They describe unique geographical features, events of historical significance, and honor pioneer residents. Here are fifty-two of them.

34. STOPS OF INTEREST IN ALBERTA Volume Two: Another fifty-four historical markers along the highways of "Wild Rose" country.

35. ELIZABETH McDOUGALL Madonna of the Plains: She was the first white woman settler in what is today Alberta. Despite a lifetime of tragedy and disappointment, she helped those in need, whether orphaned Indian children or a wandering trapper dying of tuberculosis.

36. MAGNIFICENT YELLOWHEAD HIGHWAY — Volume One: From Portage La Prairie westward 1,650 miles to the Pacific Ocean, the Yellowhead offers a panorama of prairie, plains and mountains. This volume describes 750 miles from Portage to Edmonton.

37. MAGNIFICENT YELLOWHEAD HIGHWAY — Volume Two: From Edmonton 504 miles through Jasper National Park to the sagebrush country of southern B.C.

38. MAGNIFICENT YELLOWHEAD HIGHWAY — Volume Three: From Mount Robson, the Rockies highest peak, westward 628 miles through some of North America's most scenic sport fishing country to tidewater at Prince Rupert.

39. GHOST TOWNS JOURNAL — Volume One: Old Fort Macleod, Haneyville, Boundary Creek, Taylorville, Beazer, Mountain View, Oil City and other southwestern Alberta settlements once looked optimistically to the future, but their future never came.

40. GHOST TOWNS JOURNAL — Volume Two: Pakowki, Manyberries, Brant, Bow City, Altorado, Retla, Cleverville, and similar communities in southeastern Alberta once flourished but today live mainly in old photos and the memories of a few old-timers.

Available at many retail outlets throughout B.C., Alberta, Saskatchewan and Manitoba or direct from Frontier Books, Box 1228, Station A, Surrey, B.C. V3S 2B3.